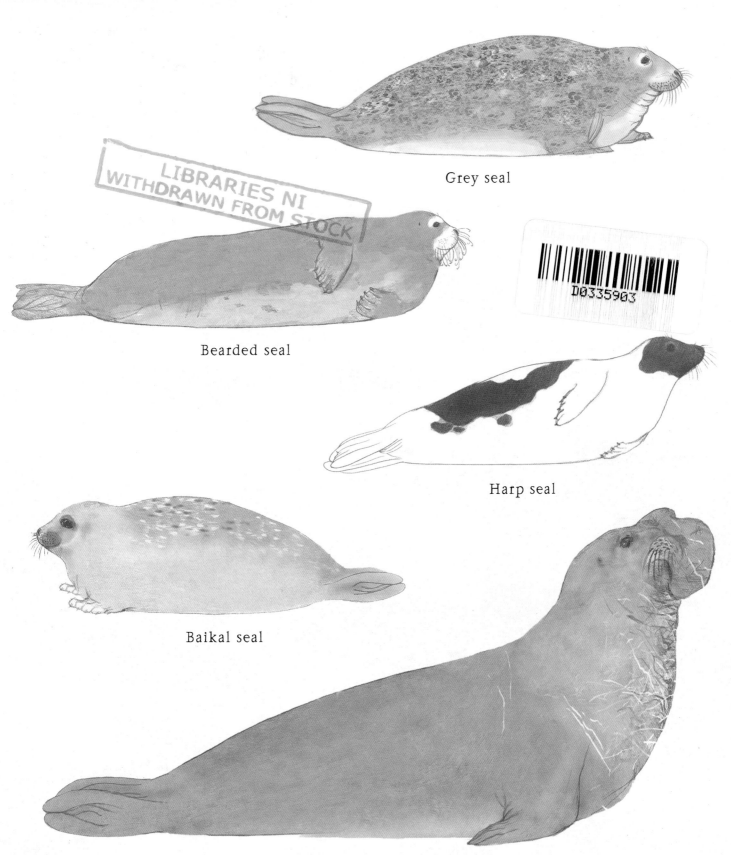

Grey seal

Bearded seal

Harp seal

Baikal seal

Northern elephant seal

For the Cornwall Seal Group
www.cornwallsealgroup.co.uk
C.B.

For my family
K.N.

The author and publisher would like to thank Sue Sayer,
founder member of the Cornwall Seal Group, for her invaluable advice
and feedback during the preparation of this book.

SEEING WILD SEALS

Seals are sea mammals – but unlike dolphins or whales, they live partly on land, coming ashore to sleep, to digest their food, to moult their fur and to pup.

So you might easily see wild seals, if you're out walking along the coast... Seals are curious, and often look as interested to see you, as you are to see them. It's wise to keep your distance though, for your own safety, as well as the seals'.

The seals you're most likely to see are "true seals". There are eighteen different kinds. The kind in this story are Grey seals, but you can see pictures of all the other true seals at either end of the book.

Grey seals used to be hunted till they almost died out. Now they are protected by law in many countries around the North Atlantic Ocean where they live. Their numbers have grown, though there are still not as many as there once were.

See What a Seal Can Do

CHRIS BUTTERWORTH

illustrated by

KATE NELMS

WALKER BOOKS
AND SUBSIDIARIES
LONDON · BOSTON · SYDNEY · AUCKLAND

If you're down by
the sea one day,
you might spot a seal,
lying about like a fat sunbather,
or flumping along the sand.

(A flump is a flop and a jump both together:
it's how a seal gets about on dry land.
It's not stylish, but it works!)

The seals in this book
are called Grey seals – or
sometimes Horsehead seals,
because of their long noses.

Seals are mammals,
like us. They are warm-blooded
and breathe air.

7

And you might think
a seal's just a slow, dozy creature
that spends its time lazing about.

But you'd be wrong!

Seal spends most of his time in the sea;
it's where he finds all his food.

Grey seals mainly eat fish that live on the seabed, especially sand eels.

He's off to look for some now...

Seals spend time together in groups on land, but they usually swim alone.

9

Splash!

A big breath out
and down he goes.
His body's just the right shape
to shoot through the water:
sleek, smooth and pointed at both ends.

When **you** dive, you have
to take a big breath **in** –
but a seal blows
its breath **out**.

His back flippers
power him
thirty metres down
in seconds.

*Seals push themselves
through the water
with their strong back
flippers, and steer
with their front flippers
and their tails.*

Seal slips through the seaweed forest –
big eyes searching the gloom.

His sharp ears hear dolphins
whistle, and a ferry-boat's
engine chugging.

Grey seals' ears are
just tiny holes behind
their eyes, yet they can
hear well underwater
and on land.

Seal's not the only
hungry one down here:
bigger things than him
are looking for their supper.

His long whiskers are his feelers:
they twitch as a silent swirl of water
tells him there's a killer whale
on the hunt for
a plump seal meal.

With a flick
and a twist of his flippers,
he dives deeper.

14

Only something
bigger and faster
than a seal
can catch it:
sharks and
killer whales
eat them.

Sixty metres down, and it's colder,
but Seal isn't bothered.

He has two fur coats that keep
him waterproof,
and a thick layer of fat under his skin
wraps him round like a duvet.

Inside his blubber, Seal's
as warm as you and me!

*Grey seals "moult" or shed
their fur every year, which
keeps their coats thick
and waterproof.*

Grey seals live only in the
cool North Atlantic,
so they need to be able
to keep warm.

Grey seals
can slow their
heartbeat, so as to
use less oxygen. It helps them dive
deeper and stay down for longer.

Ninety metres down, and
his heart gets slower ... and slower,
till it only beats four times a minute.

Seal finds most of his food down here.
He swallows a few sand eels and
waits to see what else
might turn up...

At last, even Grey seals run out of oxygen, and have to come up for air.

20

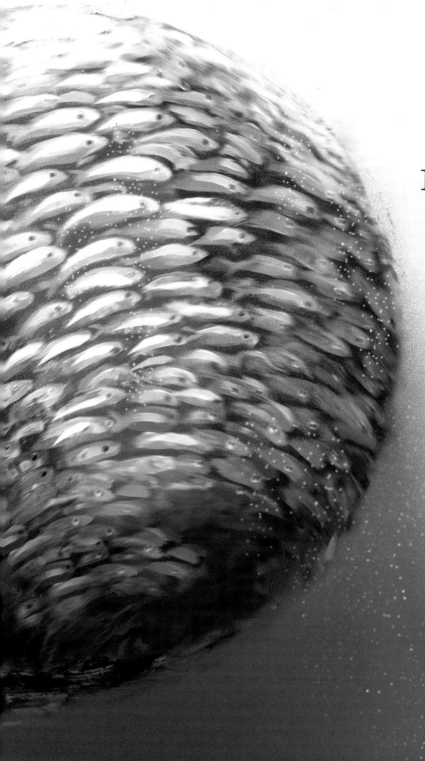

But he can't stay
this deep for ever.

Up he swims,
whiskers twitching,
ears sharp,
eyes wide –
and spies some
stragglers on
the edge of a
mackerel shoal.

Then all at once,
with a twist

and
a turn,
he's on them.

Grey seals
eat some
fish from
nearer
the surface
too.

Got one!

When Grey seals
open their mouths
to catch fish,
their throats close
so they won't
swallow water.

Pop!

It's a whole
quarter of an hour
since Seal's last
breath of fresh air.

Seals can bend like bananas to keep their noses out of chilly sea water.

Back at the seal beach,
he's too tired to play with the others.

He finds a warm rock,
yawns,
stretches,
has a good scratch ...

*Grey seals have five claws
on each front flipper – just
right for scratching!*

and falls sound asleep – still as
his rock, but snoring loudly.
zzZZZZ!

So if you're down by the sea
one day, you might spot a seal,
lying about like a fat sunbather.

And you might think he's just a slow,
dozy creature that spends his time
lazing about...

But you'd be wrong!

Seal can dive like a rocket
and twist like a dancer –
he's a super-swimming,
underwater wonder!

INDEX

Look up the pages to find out about all these seal things.
Don't forget to look at both kinds of word – **this kind** and *this kind*.

If you'd like to find out more about wild seals, here are some websites you could go to:
www.bbc.co.uk/nature   animals.nationalgeographic.com

First published 2013 by Walker Books Ltd, 87 Vauxhall Walk, London SE11 5HJ

This edition published 2014

2 4 6 8 10 9 7 5 3

Text @ 2013 Chris Butterworth Illustrations @ 2013 Kate Nelms

The right of Chris Butterworth and Kate Nelms to be identified as author and
illustrator respectively of this work has been asserted by them in accordance
with the Copyright, Designs and Patents Act 1988.

This book has been typeset in Godlike

Printed in China

978-1-4063-5270-2

www.walker.co.uk

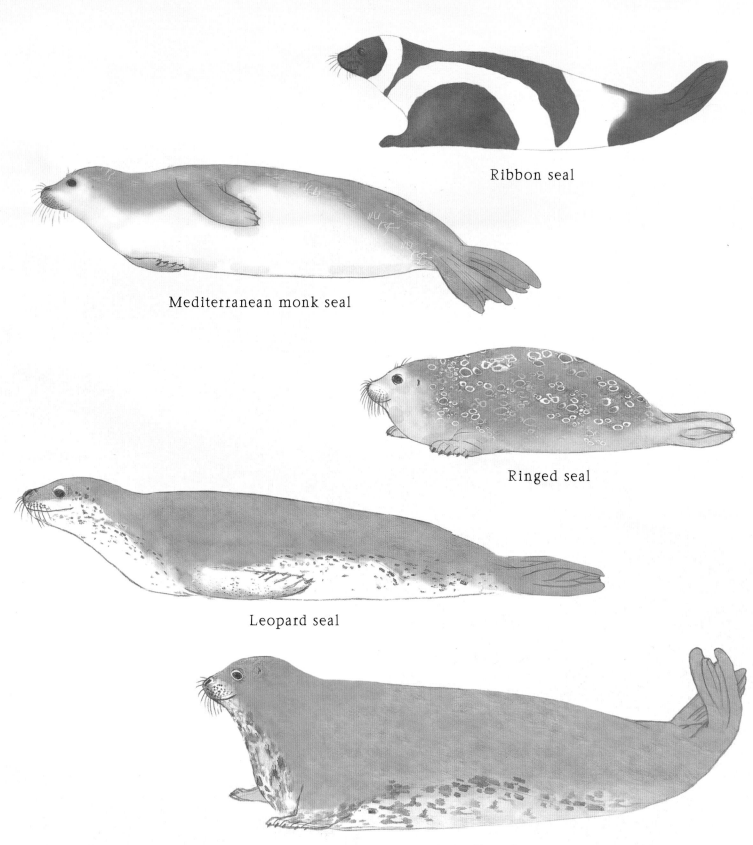

Ribbon seal

Mediterranean monk seal

Ringed seal

Leopard seal

Weddell seal

Ross seal

Southern elephant seal

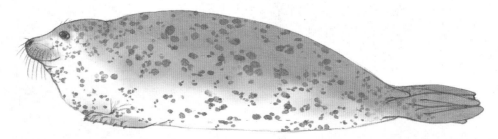

Spotted seal

Note to Parents

Sharing books with children is one of the best ways to help them learn. And it's one of the best ways they learn to read, too.

Nature Storybooks are beautifully illustrated, award-winning information picture books whose focus on animals has a strong appeal for children. They can be read as stories, revisited and enjoyed again and again, inviting children to become excited about a subject, to think and discover, and to want to find out more.

Each book is an adventure into the real world that broadens children's experience and develops their curiosity and understanding – and that's the best kind of learning there is.

Note to Teachers

Nature Storybooks provide memorable reading experiences for children in Key Stages 1 and 2 (Years 1–4), and also offer many learning opportunities for exploring a topic through words and pictures.

By working with the stories, either individually or together, children can respond to the animal world through a variety of activities, including drawing and painting, role play, talking and writing.

The books provide a rich starting-point for further research and for developing children's knowledge of information genres.

Nature Storybooks support the literacy curriculum in a variety of ways, providing:
- a focus for a whole class topic
- high-quality texts for guided reading
- a resource for the class read-aloud programme
- information texts for the class and school library for developing children's individual reading interests

Find more information on how to use Nature Storybooks in the classroom at
www.walker.co.uk/naturestorybooks

Nature Storybooks support KS 1–2 English and KS 1–2 Science